MAKING IT HAPPEN!

FIRE WIFE JOURNAL

*Standing Strong In
Your Relationship, Your Life, and
Your Dreams*

TARA McINTOSH

> "It's the soul's duty to be
> loyal to its own desires.
> It must abandon itself to its
> master passion"
>
> ~ Dame Rebecca West

WELCOME TO YOUR BRAND NEW CHAPTER

WHETHER YOU ARE growing through something in your life or are ready to start fresh, this journal is your special place to self-reflect. Use it to visualize your future, set goals, work through challenges, and (more than anything) remember how incredible you are with regular, personal celebrations. As the spouse of a firefighter, you are the one on the "other" front lines. You are also a woman with a life and dreams of her own, and it's time to honor that fact. Welcome to your *Fire Wife Journal*!

This Journal Belongs To:

_____

GROUNDING THOUGHTS & CAPTIVATING WORDS

MOTIVATING THOUGHTS AND inspiring words can lift our spirits and cheer us on. Start by choosing a special "theme" word for the year. This theme word can be something to help you focus on a trait you'd like to grow in, or just something that will keep you motivated and focused on your intent for the year.

Next, think about those quotes, philosophies, or poems that cheer, motivate, and inspire you. If you don't already have some, look to your favorite leaders, poets, writers, and artists as a starting point. What have they said or done that has captured your imagination, uplifted your day, or carried you through a tough spot?

Record those sources of inspiration here in your journal. Write them out, draw them in, cut and paste, tape them down ... get creative!

GROUNDING THOUGHTS AND CAPTIVATING WORDS

My Theme for the Year Is: _____

GROUNDING THOUGHTS AND CAPTIVATING WORDS

GROUNDING THOUGHTS AND CAPTIVATING WORDS

MY DREAM FOR ADVENTURE AND FUN

ADVENTURE AND FUN bring that spring to your step: the glow into your soul. Whether your adventures are near or far, escapade and fun is what makes life that much more riveting. What is adventure and fun to you? What would you like to try, or where would you like to go? If nothing jumps out at you right away, take some time to explore what it is you like, and decide whether you need to do more of that, or try something new instead.

Make a list of things you have loved to do in the past and would like to do more of from now on, starting now. It's time to start checking things off your bucket list.

To give you some fresh ideas of what you'd authentically like to do, take note of which books and movies you really like and why.

MY DREAM FOR ADVENTURE AND FUN

MY DREAM FOR ADVENTURE AND FUN

MY DREAM FOR ADVENTURE AND FUN

SOUL-SATISFYING FRIENDSHIPS & CONNECTIONS

WHO ARE THE magical people in and around your life? Who do you feel naturally "in sync" with and happy to be around? What connections enrich your life and leave you feeling full and satisfied?

Whether these people are your chosen family and friends, or those you just communicate with once in a while, what is it that you value about these connections? Their reciprocity? Non-judgment Fun? Trust? Encouragement? Laughter?

What groups and gatherings (online or in-person) do you love? Sunday night dinners? Jazz concerts? Book or running clubs? Cooking classes?

If you need more soul-satisfying connections, it's time to make a plan: take note of your values, what's important to you in relationships, and what activities bring you both energy and excitement.

SOUL-SATISFYING FRIENDSHIPS & CONNECTIONS

SOUL-SATISFYING FRIENDSHIPS & CONNECTIONS

SOUL-SATISFYING FRIENDSHIPS & CONNECTIONS

CREATIVE LIVING

WHETHER YOU BAKE a beautiful loaf of bread, plant a garden, paint a mural, or build a chair, the act of creating connects us to the mystery, magic, and wonder of life. Plus, it's fun to allow our imagination to wake up and run wild. Whether you want to put together photo albums or learn how to sew, creativity is at the heart and soul of who you are.

Together with your gifts, passions and interests, how you do things is unique to you and can inspire others. There is always a new and undiscovered way to do something. Think outside the box, and let your creative dreams come alive on the following pages through your words, pictures, and ideas.

CREATIVE LIVING

CREATIVE LIVING

CREATIVE LIVING

HEALTH AND WELL-BEING

YOUR HEALTH AND wellness are linked to your life's purpose: when you have energy and feel comfortable in your own skin, you will have the confidence to "run your race" and the vitality to accomplish everything you've set your heart on.

Think about your "why" for being healthy, and then map out ideas for your mind, body, and spirit. Reflect on your lifestyle habits, and then describe what boundaries you can set around you for self-care that will benefit your life and make you feel whole. Make a list of your social, emotional, and mental health needs, the foods that you love, and the exercise you enjoy.

When you take care of your health, your body will take care of you. Be patient; real, lasting change takes time. Just make small adjustments each day.

HEALTH AND WELL-BEING

HEALTH AND WELL-BEING

HEALTH AND WELL BEING

FINANCIAL SERENITY & ABUNDANCE

FINANCIAL SERENITY, AND even financial abundance, begin with the practice of gratitude. It has been said that practicing gratitude turns what you *already have* into *more*.

Reflect on your relationship to money. Where do your beliefs and feelings about money come from? Are you familiar with the laws of attraction and abundance? Without anyone else's opinions or influence, what are your authentic financial dreams? To buy a house, to travel? How can you make those dreams come true? Learn from a financial mentor or read good books on how to invest and save your money.

How about upgrading your education and skills for a career you'd like? Is there an idea you've had that you aspire to bring to life? Take time to reflect and give new energy to your financial goals. What would give you plenty, purpose, and peace?

FINANCIAL SERENITY AND ABUNDANCE

FINANCIAL SERENITY AND ABUNDANCE

FINANCIAL SERENITY AND ABUNDANCE

NO REGRETS!

HERE IS AN exercise in foresight: what must you do before you are 99 years old? What things must you accomplish or experience to make you feel as though you have lived a life well-spent? The goal for us all is to have no regrets when all is said and done.

Put together your bucket list. This should include both your short-term and long-term intentions. Remember to add rough timelines for when you want to get things done, as well as *why* these items are important to you.

NO REGRETS!

Short-Term Intentions   Timeline

NO REGRETS!

Short-Term Intentions   Timeline

NO REGRETS!

Long-Term Intentions   Timeline

MY BEST LIFE

DESCRIBE WHAT YOUR best life looks like. This is no time to hold back! What are your deepest dreams and desires? What do you hope and long for? What would you like to "build?" A family, a house, or a business? And how about character traits that you'd like to become stronger in to support your authentic self and yearnings?

One way to discover more of what you want out of life is to ask yourself, "What would I do if I could not fail and money were no object?" Also, think back to some of your best days: what made you happy and what would you like to do more of. Envision every aspect of your life and how you can unlock your potential to make your best life happen!

You are the author of your life! This is your time to dream with abandon. Think of your life with passion and fulfillment in mind. What does that look like? Let the manifestation begin!

MY BEST LIFE

MY BEST LIFE

MY BEST LIFE

AMOUR PROPRE

AMOUR PROPRE IS French for "self-respect" or "self-love." You were already born worthy and valuable, but sometimes we can lose the great truth of who we are when we believe the inaccurate labels put on us or are treated unfairly. When we don't practice self-respect, other people's fears, limitations, or unhealed wounds can rule our life and quash our light. The practice of self-love and self-respect is about making choices that make you feel good about who you are.

You can begin to bolster your amour propre with positive "I am" mantras and by setting boundaries so that others respect your needs and time. Remember what brings you pleasure and reflect on your natural gifts and talents.

Own your story, own your life and be proud of who you are!

AMOUR PROPRE

AMOUR PROPRE

AMOUR PROPRE

MY CROWN OF COURAGE

YOU WEAR IT well, your crown of courage. And while you may not be the one who runs into a burning building when everyone else is running out, you are also brave, and your history has proven this to you. Whether you stood up for a cause or trained for something that seemed impossible, it's time to take a trip down memory lane and remember all the times, big or small, when you were brave.

You have accomplished things in your life that took perseverance and determination. You have risen strong many times. You stand on the shoulders of many who came before you, and they continue to cheer you on. When you make the leap, the net will appear!

MY CROWN OF COURAGE

MY CROWN OF COURAGE

MY CROWN OF COURAGE

MY HAPPY PLACES

IT ONLY TAKES 14 seconds to change your thoughts. Sometimes your mind is in a bad place, and you need to do something to pull it out. That is what this section of your Journal is for. Think of your places far and wide, near and dear to you. Then close your eyes and imagine being there. Let your happy places bring a smile to your face.

Make a list of your happy places, be that in writing, pictures, poems, or mementos, and refer to them when needed. Always keep your happy place visions nearby if you need a little change of mood. Memory is a powerful tool; set your future self up for a rescue here with things you know will help when you need it.

MY HAPPY PLACES

MY HAPPY PLACES

MY HAPPY PLACES

MY PRIORITIES

NOW THAT WE'VE covered your dreams, goals, and sense of joy and self-worth, we can use them to determine your priorities. Record your personal top priorities here, and add pictures too! This will support you in focusing on what is important so you can accomplish what you'd like, and spend time with those you love. When you are clear about your priorities, it will remind you of what to say "yes" and what to say "no" to. Clear, articulated, measurable, *tangible* priorities will help pull wispy aspirations from the aether and solidify them into reality.

MY PRIORITIES

MY PRIORITIES

MY PRIORITIES

HAPPY BIRTHDAY, HAPPY NEW YEAR!

YOUR BIRTHDAY IS a very special day, because it's your personal new year! How would you like to mark your special anniversary? What are you dreaming of? What would you like to do this year? This is your time to write out some new goals about where you would like to go, and who you would like to become.

It is also a good time to reflect on what you loved about the past year and what you would like to change. Is there anything you'd like to let go of—habits, career, traits—that will allow you to be even better than you already are? How would you like your new year to unfold so that it's better than the last? What are you wishing for? Wishes don't have to be realistic; they can point the way at a deeper desire that is unfulfilled. Explore what your heart has been yearning for.

HAPPY BIRTHDAY, HAPPY NEW YEAR!

HAPPY BIRTHDAY, HAPPY NEW YEAR!

HAPPY BIRTHDAY, HAPPY NEW YEAR

MONTHLY GOALS AND WEEKLY WRITINGS

EACH MONTH FOR the course of six months, take the opportunity to review your goals and reflect on past events, making adjustments where needed or setting new goals to achieve. Note anything specific you would like to improve on and things you are looking forward to each month. Whether those goals are met or not, simply acknowledging them can help put order to what may be an otherwise muddled sense of things "to do."

The following pages are for you to write about anything and everything that is on your mind throughout each month through mid-year! We have included two pages per month for your goals and six pages for your weekly blessings. Don't forget to incorporate gratitude and affirm positive thoughts about your future and yourself. Set your intentions at the start of each week for what you would like to achieve.

MONTHLY GOALS AND OPPORTUNITIES FOR

_____
(MONTH)

MONTHLY GOALS AND OPPORTUNITIES FOR

_____
(MONTH)

WEEKLY WRITINGS

WEEKLY WRITINGS

WEEKLY WRITINGS

WEEKLY WRITINGS

WEEKLY WRITINGS

WEEKLY WRITINGS

MONTHLY GOALS AND OPPORTUNITIES FOR

_____
(MONTH)

MONTHLY GOALS AND OPPORTUNITIES FOR

_____
(MONTH)

WEEKLY WRITINGS

WEEKLY WRITINGS

WEEKLY WRITINGS

WEEKLY WRITINGS

WEEKLY WRITINGS

WEEKLY WRITINGS

MONTHLY GOALS AND OPPORTUNITIES FOR

_____
(MONTH)

MONTHLY GOALS AND OPPORTUNITIES FOR

_____
(MONTH)

WEEKLY WRITINGS

WEEKLY WRITINGS

WEEKLY WRITINGS

WEEKLY WRITINGS

WEEKLY WRITINGS

WEEKLY WRITINGS

MONTHLY GOALS AND OPPORTUNITIES FOR

_____
(MONTH)

MONTHLY GOALS AND OPPORTUNITIES FOR

_____
(MONTH)

WEEKLY WRITINGS

WEEKLY WRITINGS

WEEKLY WRITINGS

WEEKLY WRITINGS

WEEKLY WRITINGS

WEEKLY WRITINGS

MONTHLY GOALS AND OPPORTUNITIES FOR

_____
(MONTH)

MONTHLY GOALS AND OPPORTUNITIES FOR

_____
(MONTH)

WEEKLY WRITINGS

WEEKLY WRITINGS

WEEKLY WRITINGS

WEEKLY WRITINGS

WEEKLY WRITINGS

WEEKLY WRITINGS

MONTHLY GOALS AND OPPORTUNITIES FOR

_____
(MONTH)

MONTHLY GOALS AND OPPORTUNITIES FOR

_____
(MONTH)

WEEKLY WRITINGS

WEEKLY WRITINGS

WEEKLY WRITINGS

WEEKLY WRITINGS

WEEKLY WRITINGS

WEEKLY WRITINGS

WEEKLY WRITINGS

MID-YEAR RETROSPECT

WHETHER YOU START your journal at the beginning of the year or right smack in the middle of it, every 6 months you should take a moment to look back. Use it as a chance to recalibrate or refine any goals and resolutions as you wish. Remember to give yourself a "Well done! or a "Way-to-go!" for any progress you have made toward your dreams.

Keep in mind that life has a mind of its own, and things don't always go according to plan. Simply revamp, redo, be patient, and persist!

MID-YEAR RETROSPECT

MID-YEAR RETROSPECT

MID-YEAR RETROSPECT

MONTHLY GOALS AND WEEKLY WRITINGS

EACH MONTH FOR the next six months, take the opportunity to review your goals and reflect on past events, making adjustments where needed or setting new goals to achieve. Note anything specific you would like to improve on and things you are looking forward to each month. Whether those goals are met or not, simply acknowledging them can help put order to what may be an otherwise muddled sense of things "to do."

The following pages are for you to write about anything and everything that is on your mind throughout each month through the end of the year! We have included two pages per month for your goals and six pages for your weekly blessings. Don't forget to incorporate gratitude and affirm positive thoughts about your future and yourself. Set your intentions at the start of each week for what you would like to achieve.

MONTHLY GOALS AND OPPORTUNITIES FOR

_____
(MONTH)

MONTHLY GOALS AND OPPORTUNITIES FOR

_____
(MONTH)

WEEKLY WRITINGS

WEEKLY WRITINGS

WEEKLY WRITINGS

WEEKLY WRITINGS

WEEKLY WRITINGS

WEEKLY WRITINGS

MONTHLY GOALS AND OPPORTUNITIES FOR

_____
(MONTH)

MONTHLY GOALS AND OPPORTUNITIES FOR

_____
(MONTH)

WEEKLY WRITINGS

WEEKLY WRITINGS

WEEKLY WRITINGS

WEEKLY WRITINGS

WEEKLY WRITINGS

WEEKLY WRITINGS

MONTHLY GOALS AND OPPORTUNITIES FOR

_____
(MONTH)

MONTHLY GOALS AND OPPORTUNITIES FOR

_____
(MONTH)

WEEKLY WRITINGS

WEEKLY WRITINGS

WEEKLY WRITINGS

WEEKLY WRITINGS

WEEKLY WRITINGS

WEEKLY WRITINGS

MONTHLY GOALS AND OPPORTUNITIES FOR

_____
(MONTH)

MONTHLY GOALS AND OPPORTUNITIES FOR

_____
(MONTH)

WEEKLY WRITINGS

WEEKLY WRITINGS

WEEKLY WRITINGS

WEEKLY WRITINGS

WEEKLY WRITINGS

WEEKLY WRITINGS

MONTHLY GOALS AND OPPORTUNITIES FOR

_____
(MONTH)

MONTHLY GOALS AND OPPORTUNITIES FOR

_____
(MONTH)

WEEKLY WRITINGS

WEEKLY WRITINGS

WEEKLY WRITINGS

WEEKLY WRITINGS

WEEKLY WRITINGS

WEEKLY WRITINGS

MONTHLY GOALS AND OPPORTUNITIES FOR

_____
(MONTH)

MONTHLY GOALS AND OPPORTUNITIES FOR

_____
(MONTH)

WEEKLY WRITINGS

WEEKLY WRITINGS

WEEKLY WRITINGS

WEEKLY WRITINGS

WEEKLY WRITINGS

WEEKLY WRITINGS

WEEKLY WRITINGS

END OF YEAR RETROSPECT

THE END OF the year (whether that is a calendar year or your year journaling) is a sacred time to curl up and honor the time that has passed and reflect on what it meant. Writer Zora Neale Hurston once said, "There are years that ask questions, and years that answer." Which one was it for you?

As you take the time to reflect on the past year, also take the time to reflect on the upcoming one, too. What do you hope for? What are you dreaming about? What would you like to change? Take in the lessons and the memories of the past year. Then, in your new year, plant more of what you want and prune away all that you don't.

It's time to write your new chapter.

END OF YEAR RETROSPECT

END OF YEAR RETROSPECT

END OF YEAR RETROSPECT

WRITING YOUR NEW CHAPTER

BEFORE YOU START your brand-new Fire Wife Journal for the upcoming year, use this section as part of your end of the year retrospect to brainstorm your most elaborate intentions, ideas and dreams! Feel free to doodle, make lists, draw pictures, and just be random. You can also use an oracle card deck and record any other inspirational messages that can help you formulate new ideas and broaden your perspective. You have four pages in this section to just do your thing—Go for it!

WRITING YOUR NEW CHAPTER

WRITING YOUR NEW CHAPTER

WRITING YOUR NEW CHAPTER

OTHER BOOKS BY
TARA McINTOSH

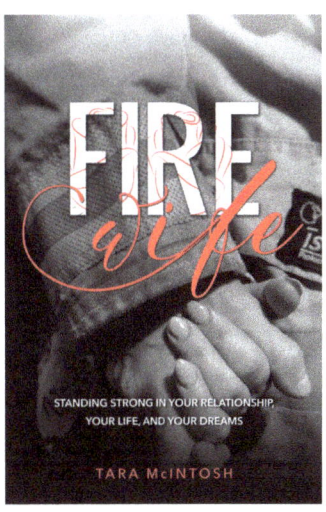 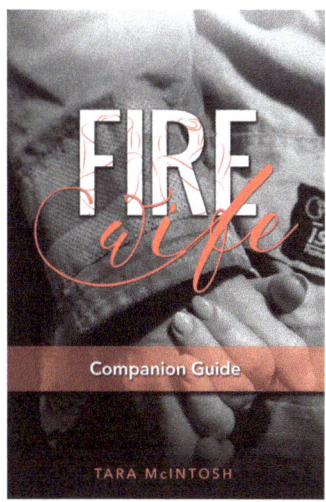

Let's stay connected! Come and join our community at
www.firewifewise.com
for articles on Fire Life, starting a Fire Wife book club,
recipes and more!

www.ingramcontent.com/pod-product-compliance
Lightning Source LLC
Chambersburg PA
CBHW040423100526
44589CB00022B/2811